Table of Contents

Unit 1—Concepts of Print

Unit 2—Phonemic Awareness

Unit 3—Alphabet Awareness

Unit 4—Sound Symbol Awareness

Unit 5—Vocabulary and Concept Development

Unit 6—Comprehension

As Easy as 1–2–3

1 **Prepare** the assessment task activity.

2 **Administer** the task and record the student's performance.

3 **Reteach** or provide additional practice using the reproducible activity sheet.

Everything You Need

Each assessment task includes:

- **Scripted instructions**
  for administering the assessment task

- **Full-color mats and cards**
  to engage the student in a specific task

- **Class checklist**
  to record each student's performance

- **Reproducible activity sheets**
  for additional skill practice

When to Conduct an Assessment

You may choose to use assessment tasks in any of the following ways:

- Assess students at the beginning of the school year to determine individual student skill levels.

- Administer an assessment after a specific skill has been taught to help confirm mastery or need for further instruction.

- Assess students throughout the year to monitor progress. Use the correlation chart on page 6 to correlate assessments with your lesson plans.

You may also wish to visit www.teaching-standards.com to view how the skills are correlated to your state's standards.

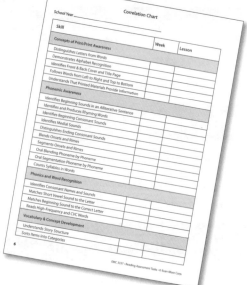

Preparing an Assessment Task Activity

Assemble each assessment task activity and place it in an envelope.
Store the envelopes in a file box or crate for easy access.

Materials:

- 9" x 12" (23 x 30.5 cm) large manila envelopes
- scissors
- clear tape
- scripted instructions, manipulatives, class checklist, and activity sheet for the specific assessment task

Steps to Follow:

1. Remove and laminate the *scripted instruction page*. Tape it to the front of the envelope.

2. Remove and laminate the *manipulatives* (sorting mats, task cards, etc.). Store cards in a smaller envelope or plastic bag.

3. Reproduce the *class checklist*. Tape it to the back of the envelope.

4. Make multiple copies of the *activity sheet* and store them in the envelope.

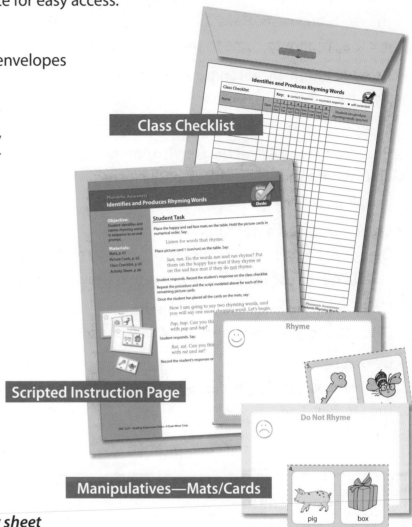

Class Checklist

Scripted Instruction Page

Manipulatives—Mats/Cards

Make one copy of the *Individual Student Assessment Checklist* (page 5) for each student in your class. You may wish to keep these checklists in a separate binder so they are easily referenced.

Activity Sheet

How to Conduct an Assessment

- **Be prepared.**
Preread the scripted instructions. Follow the directions at the top of the script for setting out the cards and mats. Have the class checklist at hand to record the student's responses. Do not ask the student to come to the table until all task materials are in place.

- **Provide a non-threatening atmosphere.**
The student should complete the task at a quiet, isolated table. Refer to the activity as a "task" or "job," not as a "test."

- **Provide a non-distracting environment.**
The student should be able to easily focus on the task. Sit next to the student. Communicate in a clear, concise way.

- **Be an unbiased assessor.**
Do not encourage or discourage or approve or disapprove of the student's responses. Be careful not to use facial expressions that provide feedback.

- **Know when to stop the assessment.**
Discontinue the assessment activity if it becomes obvious that the student cannot do the task.

- **Be discreet.**
When recording the student's responses, keep the checklist close to you so it will not distract the student.

What does this mean?

/p/	When a letter is between / /, the letter sound, not the letter name, should be pronounced.
c•at	When a bullet appears within a word, emphasize each word part separately.
(ˇ)	is used to represent short vowel sounds: căt, gĕt, ĭt, hŏt, pŭp.
(−)	is used to represent long vowel sounds: cāke, mē, bīte, hōme, ūse.
Auditory Only	Some tasks are auditory only, and are indicated by this icon on the teacher script page. Auditory tasks do not contain mats or task cards.

Individual Student Assessment Checklist

Name _____   School Year _____

Skill	Dates Tested	Date Mastered
Unit 1—Concepts of Print		
Book Awareness		
Identifies Pictures, Letters, and Words		
Understands That Printed Materials Provide Information		
Follows Words from Left to Right and Top to Bottom		
Unit 2—Phonemic Awareness		
Identifies Words That Rhyme		
Identifies Word That Does Not Rhyme		
Supplies the Missing Rhyme		
Identifies Letter Sounds at the Beginning of Words		
Identifies Letter Sounds at the End of Words		
Counts Syllables in a Word		
Unit 3—Alphabet Awareness		
Names Alphabet in Sequence		
Matches All Uppercase and Lowercase Letters		
Unit 4—Sound Symbol Awareness		
Identifies Letter and Sound		
Matches Beginning Sound and Letter		
Unit 5—Vocabulary and Concept Development		
Demonstrates Basic Knowledge		
Categorizes Objects		
Understands Positional Words		
Unit 6—Comprehension		
Understands Story Structure		
Sequences a Story		

Correlation Chart

School Year _____

Skill	Week	Lesson
Unit 1—Concepts of Print		
Book Awareness		
Identifies Pictures, Letters, and Words		
Understands That Printed Materials Provide Information		
Follows Words from Left to Right and Top to Bottom		
Unit 2—Phonemic Awareness		
Identifies Words That Rhyme		
Identifies Word That Does Not Rhyme		
Supplies the Missing Rhyme		
Identifies Letter Sounds at the Beginning of Words		
Identifies Letter Sounds at the End of Words		
Counts Syllables in a Word		
Unit 3—Alphabet Awareness		
Names Alphabet in Sequence		
Matches All Uppercase and Lowercase Letters		
Unit 4—Sound Symbol Awareness		
Identifies Letter and Sound		
Matches Beginning Sound and Letter		
Unit 5—Vocabulary and Concept Development		
Demonstrates Basic Knowledge		
Categorizes Objects		
Understands Positional Words		
Unit 6—Comprehension		
Understands Story Structure		
Sequences a Story		

   EMC 3336 • Reading Assessment Tasks • © Evan-Moor Corp.

Quick **Checks**

Unit 1
Concepts of Print

Objective:
Students show book awareness.

Materials:
Class Checklist, p. 11

Activity Sheet, p. 12

A Book from Classroom Library

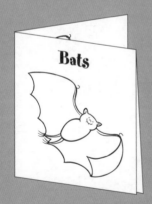

Student Task

Place the book on the table in a sideways position. Say:

> I want you to pick up this book and show me how you would hold it if you were reading it.

Student responds. Record the student's response on the class checklist. Say:

> Now I want you to open the book and look at the pictures. Keep turning the pages until you get to the end of the book.

Record the student's response on the class checklist. Open the book to a page that has text on both pages and lay it on the table. Say:

> Now show me where I would start to read.

Student responds by pointing to the text and following it from left to right. Record the student's response on the class checklist.

Book Awareness

Class Checklist		Key: + correct response – incorrect response ● self-corrected			
Name	Date	Holds Book Right Side Up	Turns Pages Front to Back	Uses Left-to-Right Directionality	Notes

Name _____

A Little Book

I see one bat.
I see one big bat.

I see three bats.
I see three little bats.

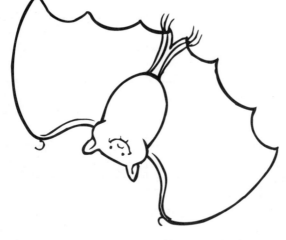

fold 2

fold 1

fold 1

Bats

I see big and little bats,
hanging upside down.

fold 2

Objective:
Student identifies pictures, letters, and words.

Materials:
Cards, pp. 15 and 17

Class Checklist, p. 19

Activity Sheet, p. 20

Student Task

Place the cards faceup in rows on the table. Say:

> Look at the cards. Pick up a card that shows one letter.

Student responds. Record the student's response on the class checklist. Say:

> Now pick up the other cards that show one letter.

Student responds. Record the student's response on the class checklist. Take the letter cards from the student. Say:

> Pick up all the cards that show a picture.

Student responds. Record the student's response on the class checklist. Take the picture cards from the student. Say:

> Now pick up all the cards that have words on them.

Student responds. Record the student's response on the class checklist. Not all the cards will be used.

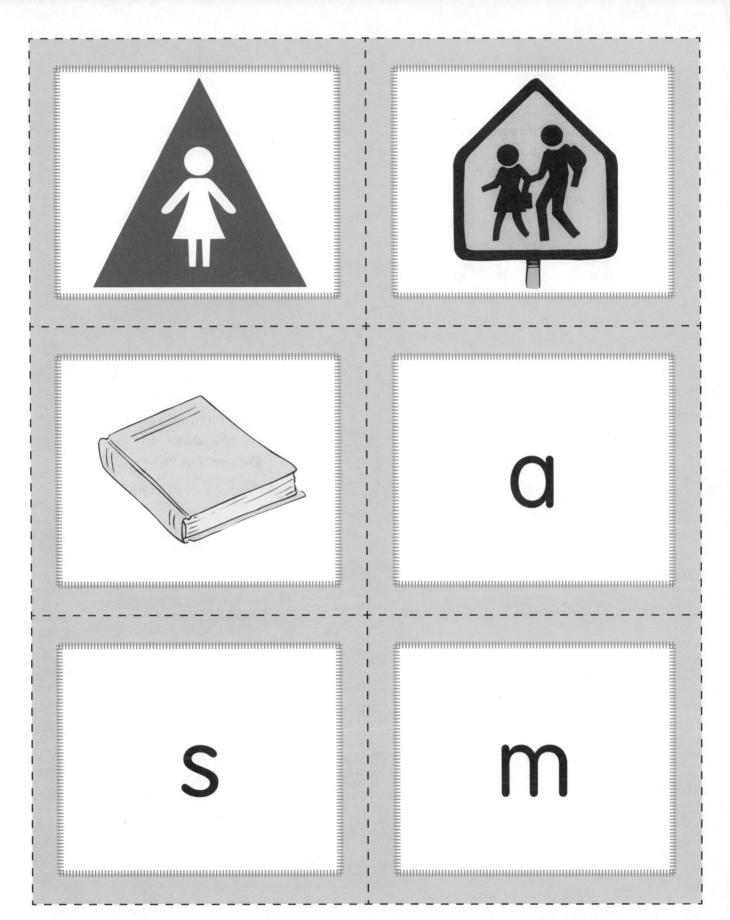

**Identifies Pictures, Letters,
and Words**

Concepts of Print

EMC 3336 • © Evan-Moor Corp.

**Identifies Pictures, Letters,
and Words**

Concepts of Print

EMC 3336 • © Evan-Moor Corp.

**Identifies Pictures, Letters,
and Words**

Concepts of Print

EMC 3336 • © Evan-Moor Corp.

**Identifies Pictures, Letters,
and Words**

Concepts of Print

EMC 3336 • © Evan-Moor Corp.

**Identifies Pictures, Letters,
and Words**

Concepts of Print

EMC 3336 • © Evan-Moor Corp.

**Identifies Pictures, Letters,
and Words**

Concepts of Print

EMC 3336 • © Evan-Moor Corp.

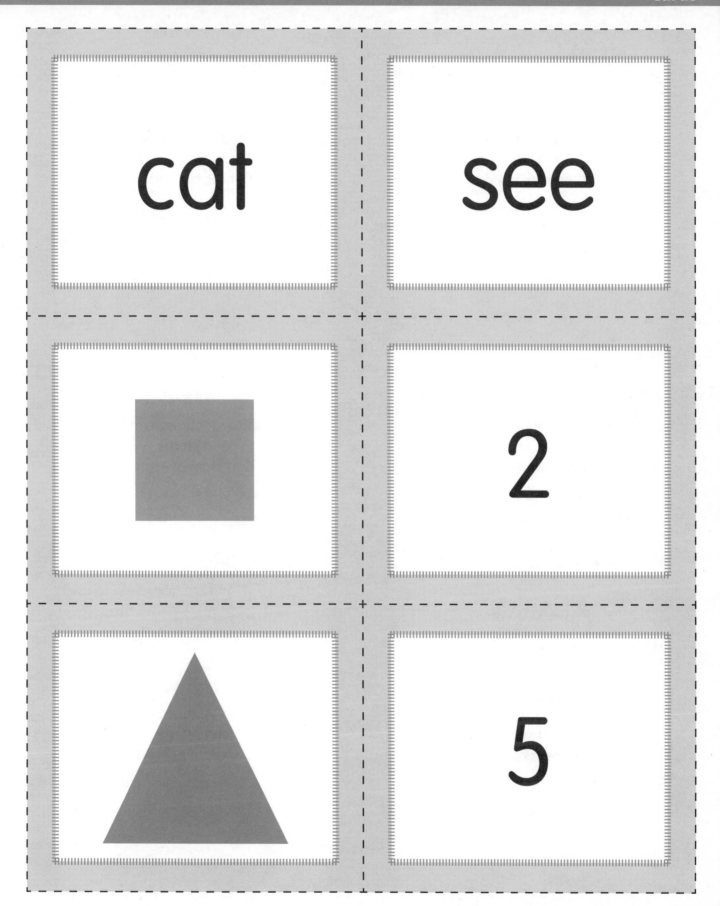

**Identifies Pictures, Letters,
and Words**
Concepts of Print

EMC 3336 • © Evan-Moor Corp.

**Identifies Pictures, Letters,
and Words**
Concepts of Print

EMC 3336 • © Evan-Moor Corp.

**Identifies Pictures, Letters,
and Words**
Concepts of Print

EMC 3336 • © Evan-Moor Corp.

**Identifies Pictures, Letters,
and Words**
Concepts of Print

EMC 3336 • © Evan-Moor Corp.

**Identifies Pictures, Letters,
and Words**
Concepts of Print

EMC 3336 • © Evan-Moor Corp.

**Identifies Pictures, Letters,
and Words**
Concepts of Print

EMC 3336 • © Evan-Moor Corp.

Identifies Pictures, Letters, and Words

Class Checklist		Key: + correct response − incorrect response • self-corrected			
Name	Date	**Letters** a, s, m	**Pictures** Bathroom Sign Crosswalk Sign Book	**Words** cat see	Notes

Name _____

Find It!

Circle the words. Underline the letters. Color the shapes.

Understands That Printed Materials Provide Information

Objective:

Student demonstrates an understanding that printed materials provide information.

Materials:

Cards, p. 23

Class Checklist, p. 25

Activity Sheet, p. 26

Student Task

Place the brown dog card on the table. Say:

> Look at the card. It says *brown dog*. What do the words tell us about the dog?

Student responds. (Sample response: *The dog is brown.*) Record the student's response on the class checklist. Remove the brown dog card and place the blue bird card on the table. Say:

> Look at the card. It says *little blue bird*. What do the words tell us about the bird?

Student responds. (Sample response: *The little bird is blue.*) Record the student's response on the class checklist. Remove the blue bird card and place the red wagon card on the table. Say:

> Look at the card. It says *fast red wagon*. What do the words tell us about the wagon?

Student responds. (Sample response: *The wagon is fast and red.*) Record the student's response on the class checklist. Remove the red wagon card and place the yellow sun card on the table. Say:

> Look at the card. It says *yellow sun*. What do the words tell us about the sun?

Student responds. (Sample response: *The sun is yellow.*) Record the student's response on the class checklist.

brown dog

little
blue bird

fast red
wagon

yellow
sun

**Understands That Printed Materials
Provide Information**
Concepts of Print

EMC 3336 • © Evan-Moor Corp.

**Understands That Printed Materials
Provide Information**
Concepts of Print

EMC 3336 • © Evan-Moor Corp.

**Understands That Printed Materials
Provide Information**
Concepts of Print

EMC 3336 • © Evan-Moor Corp.

**Understands That Printed Materials
Provide Information**
Concepts of Print

EMC 3336 • © Evan-Moor Corp.

Understands That Printed Materials Provide Information

| Class Checklist | | Key: + correct response   − incorrect response
Record a reasonable response as a correct response. | | | | |

Name	Date	Brown Dog	Little Blue Bird	Fast Red Wagon	Yellow Sun	Notes

Name _____

Color

Listen. Follow the directions and color.

Follows Words from Left to Right and Top to Bottom

Quick
Checks

Objective:

Student demonstrates an understanding that words are read from left to right and that lines of text are read from top to bottom on a page.

Materials:

Mat 1, p. 29

Mat 2, p. 31

Class Checklist, p. 33

Activity Sheet, p. 34

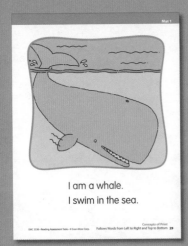

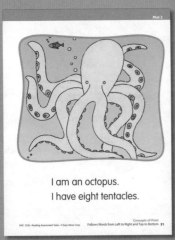

Student Task

Place either mat 1 or mat 2 on the table. Say:

> Look at the picture and the story. Point to where I should start reading.

Student responds. Say:

> Use your finger to show me which words I will read next.

Student responds. Record the student's response on the class checklist. Say:

> Once I read here (point to the end of the first sentence), then where do I read?

Student responds. Record the student's response on the class checklist.

You may wish to use the remaining mat for retesting purposes.

I am a whale.
I swim in the sea.

Concepts of Print
Follows Words from Left to Right and Top to Bottom **29**

Follows Words from Left to Right and Top to Bottom

Concepts of Print

EMC 3336 • © Evan-Moor Corp.

I am an octopus.
I have eight tentacles.

Follows Words from Left to Right and Top to Bottom

Concepts of Print

EMC 3336 • © Evan-Moor Corp.

Follows Words from Left to Right and Top to Bottom

Class Checklist		Key: **+** correct response **−** incorrect response **●** self-corrected		
Name	Date	Follows Words from Left to Right	Follows Words from Top to Bottom	Notes

Name _____

A Family

Color the picture.

We are a family.
We like to spend time together.

Quick Checks

Unit 2
Phonemic Awareness

Objective:
Student identifies words that rhyme.

Materials:
Mat, p. 39

Class Checklist, p. 41

Activity Sheet, p. 42

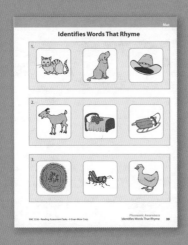

Student Task

Place the mat on the table. Point to row 1. Say:

> Look at the pictures in row 1. Listen as I name each picture. Tell me which words rhyme.
>
> *Cat, dog, hat.*

Student responds. Record the student's response on the class checklist. Say:

> Now let's look at the pictures in row 2. Tell me which words rhyme.
>
> *Goat, bed, sled.*

Student responds. Record the student's response on the class checklist. Say:

> Look at row 3. Listen as I name each picture. Tell me which words rhyme.
>
> *Rug, bug, duck.*

Student responds. Record the student's response on the class checklist.

Identifies Words That Rhyme

1.

2.

3.

Identifies Words That Rhyme

Phonemic Awareness

EMC 3336 • © Evan-Moor Corp.

Identifies Words That Rhyme

Class Checklist		Key: + correct response – incorrect response ● self-corrected			
Name	Date	cat hat	bed sled	rug bug	Notes

Name _____

Rhyming Pairs

Name the pictures in each box.
Color ☺ if the pictures rhyme.
Color ☹ if the pictures do <u>not</u> rhyme.

Identifies Word That Does Not Rhyme

Objective:
Student identifies the word that does not rhyme.

Materials:
Mat, p. 45

Class Checklist, p. 47

Activity Sheet, p. 48

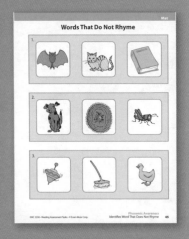

Student Task

Place the mat on the table. Point to row 1. Say:

> Look at the pictures in row 1. Listen as I name each picture. Tell me which word does not rhyme.

> *Bat, cat, book.*

Student responds. Record the student's response on the class checklist. Point to row 2. Say:

> Now look at row 2. Listen as I name each picture. Tell me which word does not rhyme.

> *Dog, rug, bug.*

Student responds. Record the student's response on the class checklist. Say:

> Look at row 3. Tell me which word does not rhyme.

> *Top, mop, duck.*

Student responds. Record the student's response on the class checklist.

Words That Do Not Rhyme

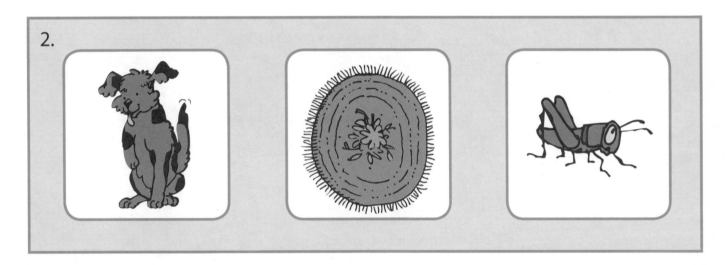

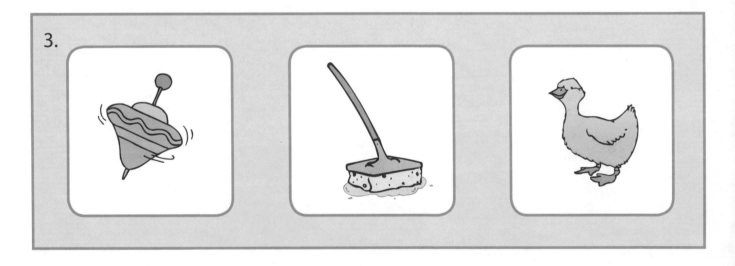

Phonemic Awareness
Identifies Word That Does Not Rhyme

Identifies Word That Does Not Rhyme

Phonemic Awareness

EMC 3336 • © Evan-Moor Corp.

Identifies Word That Does Not Rhyme

Class Checklist		Key: + correct response		– incorrect response	● self-corrected
Name	Date	Book	Dog	Duck	Notes

Note: Student circles the word in each row that does not rhyme.
1. boat, duck, goat. 2. dog, frog, fish. 3. pig, bed, sled. 4. cat, sun, bat.

Activity Sheet

Name _____

It Does Not Rhyme

Name each picture. Circle the picture in each row that does <u>not</u> rhyme.

1.

2.

3.

4.

Supplies the Missing Rhyme

Checks

Objective:

Student supplies the missing rhyming word.

Materials:

Rhyme Cards, pp. 51 and 53

Picture Cards, p. 55

Class Checklist, p. 57

Activity Sheet, p. 58

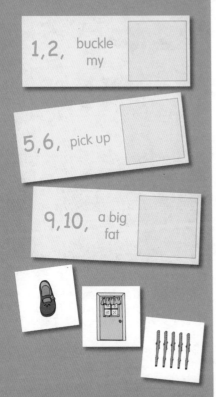

Student Task

Put the rhyme cards in order numerically and place them in a pile on the table. Spread out the picture cards faceup on the table. Place rhyme card 1, 2 on the table. Say:

> You will listen to a rhyme and pick the picture card that finishes the rhyme. Let's begin.
>
> 1, 2, buckle my _____.
> Choose the picture that rhymes with *two* and place it on the rhyme card.

Student responds. Record the student's response on the class checklist. Place the next rhyme card on the table in front of the student. Say:

> 3, 4, shut the _____.
> Choose the picture that rhymes with *four* and place it on the rhyme card.

Record the student's response on the class checklist. Place the next rhyme card on the table in front of the student. Say:

> 5, 6, pick up _____.
> Choose the picture that rhymes with *six* and place it on the rhyme card.

Record the student's response on the class checklist. Place the next rhyme card on the table in front of the student. Say:

> 7, 8, lay them _____.
> Choose the picture that rhymes with *eight* and place it on the rhyme card.

Record the student's response on the class checklist. Place the next rhyme card on the table in front of the student. Say:

> 9, 10, a big fat _____.
> Choose the picture that rhymes with *ten* and place it on the rhyme card.

Record the student's response on the class checklist.

1,2, buckle my

3,4, shut the

5,6, pick up

Phonemic Awareness
Supplies the Missing Rhyme   **51**

Supplies the Missing Rhyme
Phonemic Awareness

EMC 3336 • © Evan-Moor Corp.

Supplies the Missing Rhyme
Phonemic Awareness

EMC 3336 • © Evan-Moor Corp.

Supplies the Missing Rhyme
Phonemic Awareness

EMC 3336 • © Evan-Moor Corp.

7, 8, lay
them

9, 10, a big
fat

Supplies the Missing Rhyme

Phonemic Awareness

EMC 3336 • © Evan-Moor Corp.

Supplies the Missing Rhyme

Phonemic Awareness

EMC 3336 • © Evan-Moor Corp.

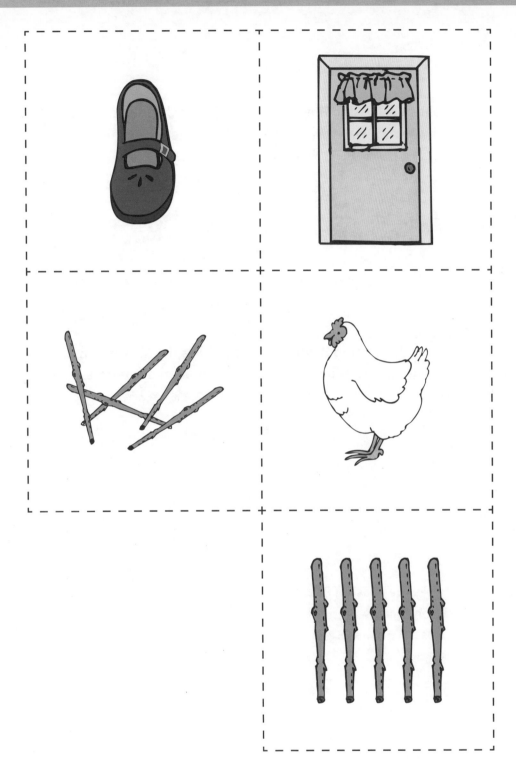

Supplies the Missing Rhyme

Phonemic Awareness

EMC 3336 • © Evan-Moor Corp.

Supplies the Missing Rhyme

Phonemic Awareness

EMC 3336 • © Evan-Moor Corp.

Supplies the Missing Rhyme

Phonemic Awareness

EMC 3336 • © Evan-Moor Corp.

Supplies the Missing Rhyme

Phonemic Awareness

EMC 3336 • © Evan-Moor Corp.

Supplies the Missing Rhyme

Phonemic Awareness

EMC 3336 • © Evan-Moor Corp.

Supplies the Missing Rhyme

Class Checklist		Key: **+** correct response − incorrect response ● self-corrected					
Name	Date	shoe	door	sticks	straight	hen	Notes

Note: Student cuts and glues the pictures to complete the rhyme.

Name _____

1, 2, Buckle My Shoe

Cut out and glue to make a rhyme.

1 2

glue

3 4

glue

5 6

glue

7 8

glue

9 10

glue

sticks

hen

shoe

door

straight

Identifies Letter Sounds at the Beginning of Words

Objective:
Student identifies the beginning sound in a given word.

Materials:
Picture Cards, p. 61
Class Checklist, p. 63
Activity Sheet, p. 64

Student Task

Place picture card 1 on the table. Say:

> Listen as I name each picture. Say the sound you hear at the beginning.
>
> *Bed, bug.*
>
> Say the sound you hear at the beginning of *bed* and *bug*.

Student responds /b/. Record the student's response on the class checklist. Place picture card 2 on the table. Say:

> *Car, corn.*
>
> Say the sound you hear at the beginning of *car* and *corn*.

Student responds /c/. Record the student's response on the class checklist. Place picture card 3 on the table. Say:

> *Soap, sun.*
>
> Say the sound you hear at the beginning of *soap* and *sun*.

Student responds /s/. Record the student's response on the class checklist. Place picture card 4 on the table. Say:

> *Map, mouse.*
>
> Say the sound you hear at the beginning of *map* and *mouse*.

Student responds /m/. Record the student's response on the class checklist.

1.

2.

3.

4.

Phonemic Awareness
Identifies Letter Sounds at the Beginning of Words   **61**

Identifies Letter Sounds at the Beginning of Words

Phonemic Awareness

EMC 3336 • © Evan-Moor Corp.

Identifies Letter Sounds at the Beginning of Words

Phonemic Awareness

EMC 3336 • © Evan-Moor Corp.

Identifies Letter Sounds at the Beginning of Words

Phonemic Awareness

EMC 3336 • © Evan-Moor Corp.

Identifies Letter Sounds at the Beginning of Words

Phonemic Awareness

EMC 3336 • © Evan-Moor Corp.

Identifies Letter Sounds at the Beginning of Words

Class Checklist		Key: + correct response − incorrect response ● self-corrected				
Name	Date	bed, bug /b/	car, corn /c/	soap, sun /s/	map, mouse /m/	Notes

Phonemic Awareness

Name _____

Same Sound

Color the picture that has the same beginning sound as the first picture.

1.

2.

3.

4.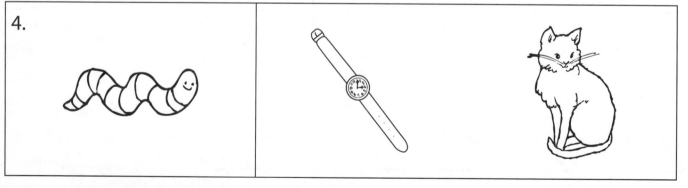

Identifies Letter Sounds at the End of Words

Objective:
Student identifies the ending sound in a given word.

Materials:
Picture Cards, p. 67

Class Checklist, p. 69

Activity Sheet, p. 70

Student Task

Place picture card 1 on the table. Say:

> Listen as I name each picture. Say the sound you hear at the end.
>
> *Foot, hat.*
>
> Say the sound you hear at the end of *foot* and *hat*.

Student responds /t/. Record the student's response on the class checklist. Place picture card 2 on the table. Say:

> *Bus, dress.*
>
> Say the sound you hear at the end of *bus* and *dress*.

Student responds /s/. Record the student's response on the class checklist. Place picture card 3 on the table. Say:

> *Pig, frog.*
>
> Say the sound you hear at the end of *pig* and *frog*.

Student responds /g/. Record the student's response on the class checklist. Place picture card 4 on the table. Say:

> *Bird, hand.*
>
> Say the sound you hear at the end of *bird* and *hand*.

Student responds /d/. Record the student's response on the class checklist.

1.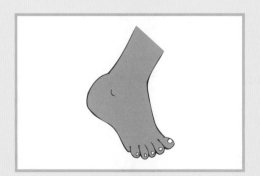

2.

3.

4.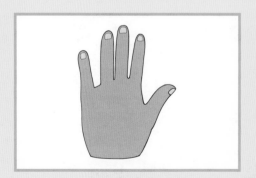

Phonemic Awareness
Identifies Letter Sounds at the End of Words

Identifies Letter Sounds at the End of Words

Phonemic Awareness

EMC 3336 • © Evan-Moor Corp.

Identifies Letter Sounds at the End of Words

Phonemic Awareness

EMC 3336 • © Evan-Moor Corp.

Identifies Letter Sounds at the End of Words

Phonemic Awareness

EMC 3336 • © Evan-Moor Corp.

Identifies Letter Sounds at the End of Words

Phonemic Awareness

EMC 3336 • © Evan-Moor Corp.

Identifies Letter Sounds at the End of Words

Class Checklist		Key:	+ correct response	− incorrect response	• self-corrected	
Name	Date	foot, hat /t/	bus, dress /s/	pig, frog /g/	bird, hand /d/	Notes

Note: Student identifies ending sounds.
1. cat, van, bat. 2. hand, bird, sun. 3. bus, duck, glass. 4. pig, top, frog.

Name _____

How Does It End?

Color the picture that has the same ending sound as the first picture.

1.

2.

3.

4.

Counts Syllables in a Word

Objective:
Student counts the number of syllables in a given word.

Materials:
Picture Cards, p. 73
Class Checklist, p. 75
Activity Sheet, p. 76

Model the Task

Put the picture cards in numerical order. Say:

> Today we are going to count parts of words.

Place the picture of the airplane on the table. Say:

> *Air•plane.* I hear two parts in the word *airplane.*

Student Task

Place the kitten picture card on the table. Say:

> *Kit•ten.* How many parts do you hear in *kitten?*

Student responds. Record the student's response on the class checklist. Place the turtle picture card on the table. Say:

> *Tur•tle.* How many parts do you hear in *turtle?*

Record the student's response on the class checklist. Place the key picture card on the table. Say:

> *Key.* How many parts do you hear in *key?*

Record the student's response on the class checklist. Place the wagon picture card on the table. Say:

> *Wa•gon.* How many parts do you hear in *wagon?*

Record the student's response on the class checklist. Place the hammer picture card on the table. Say:

> *Ham•mer.* How many parts do you hear in *hammer?*

Record the student's response on the class checklist.

Phonemic Awareness
Counts Syllables in a Word

1.

2.

3.

4.

5.

6.

Counts Syllables in a Word

Phonemic Awareness

EMC 3336 • © Evan-Moor Corp.

Counts Syllables in a Word

Phonemic Awareness

EMC 3336 • © Evan-Moor Corp.

Counts Syllables in a Word

Phonemic Awareness

EMC 3336 • © Evan-Moor Corp.

Counts Syllables in a Word

Phonemic Awareness

EMC 3336 • © Evan-Moor Corp.

Counts Syllables in a Word

Phonemic Awareness

EMC 3336 • © Evan-Moor Corp.

Counts Syllables in a Word

Phonemic Awareness

EMC 3336 • © Evan-Moor Corp.

Counts Syllables in a Word

Class Checklist		**Key:** + correct response − incorrect response ● self-corrected					
Name	Date	Kitten (2)	Turtle (2)	Key (1)	Wagon (2)	Hammer (2)	Notes

Name _____

Count It!

Name each picture. Count how many parts you hear.
Fill in the circles to show how many parts you hear.

○ ○ ○   ○ ○ ○

○ ○ ○   ○ ○ ○

○ ○ ○   ○ ○ ○

Unit 3
Alphabet Awareness

Names Alphabet in Sequence

Quick Checks

Objective:
Student names uppercase and lowercase letters of the alphabet in sequence.

Materials:
Mats, pp. 81 and 83

Class Checklist, p. 85

Activity Sheet, p. 86

Student Task

Place the lowercase alphabet mat on the table. Use a piece of paper or a ruler to isolate each alphabet row. Say:

> Today we are going to name all the letters in the alphabet. First we will name all the lowercase letters.

Isolate the first row on the mat. Say:

> When I point to the letter, you say the name.

Point to the letter *a*. Allow the student time to say the letter's name before moving on to the next letter.

Continue pointing to each letter and isolating each row. Record any letters the student does not name correctly on the class checklist.

Once the student has completed naming all the lowercase letters, place the uppercase letter mat on the table. Say:

> Now we will name all the uppercase letters. Let's begin.

Isolate the first row on the mat. Continue the assessment until the student has named all the letters on the mat. Record any letters the student does not name correctly on the class checklist.

The Alphabet

a	b	c	d	e
f	g	h	i	j
k	l	m	n	o
p	q	r	s	t
u	v	w	x	y
z				

Alphabet Awareness
Names Alphabet in Sequence

Names Alphabet in Sequence

Alphabet Awareness

EMC 3336 • © Evan-Moor Corp.

The Alphabet

A	B	C	D	E
F	G	H	I	J
K	L	M	N	O
P	Q	R	S	T
U	V	W	X	Y
Z				

Alphabet Awareness
Names Alphabet in Sequence

Names Alphabet in Sequence

Alphabet Awareness

EMC 3336 • © Evan-Moor Corp.

Names Alphabet in Sequence

Class Checklist		Record any letters the student incorrectly named.	
Name	Date	Incorrectly Named Letters	Notes

Alphabet Awareness
Names Alphabet in Sequence

Note: Student practices naming ABCs aloud.

Name _____

I Know My ABCs

Point to each letter. Say the name.

Aa   Bb   Cc   Dd

Ee   Ff   Gg   Hh

Ii   Jj   Kk   Ll   Mm

Nn   Oo   Pp   Qq

Rr   Ss   Tt   Uu   Vv

Ww   Xx   Yy   Zz

Matches All Uppercase and Lowercase Letters

Quick Checks

Objective:
Student matches all uppercase letters to lowercase letters.

Materials:
Alphabet Cards, pp. 89–95

Class Checklist, p. 97

Activity Sheet, p. 98

Model the Task

Spread out alphabet cards a–h in random order on the table. Say:

> Look at the alphabet cards. There are uppercase letters and lowercase letters. I will match an uppercase letter to its lowercase letter.

Choose an uppercase letter and match it to its lowercase letter. Say the name of the letter aloud. Then as you fit them together, say:

> They fit together like a puzzle.

Student Task

> Now it's your turn. Put together an uppercase letter and a lowercase letter.

Student responds. Say:

> Which letter did you match?

Student responds.

> Make another match. Tell me the name of the letter.

Student responds.

> Keep matching all the uppercase letters to the lowercase letters. Tell me the name of the letter every time you make a match.

Once the student has matched all the letter pairs, place letters i–p in random order on the table. Once those letter pairs are matched, place q–z on the table.

Record any letters that are not matched correctly on the class checklist.

Alphabet Awareness

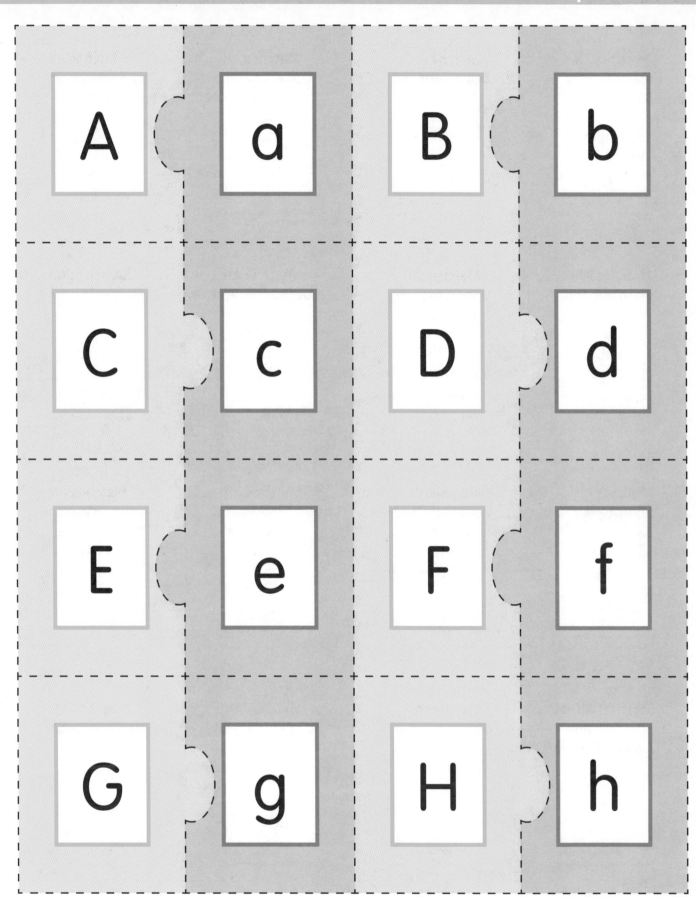

Alphabet Awareness
Matches All Uppercase and Lowercase Letters

**Matches All
Uppercase and
Lowercase
Letters**

Alphabet
Awareness

EMC 3336

© Evan-Moor Corp.

**Matches All
Uppercase and
Lowercase
Letters**

Alphabet
Awareness

EMC 3336

© Evan-Moor Corp.

**Matches All
Uppercase and
Lowercase
Letters**

Alphabet
Awareness

EMC 3336

© Evan-Moor Corp.

**Matches All
Uppercase and
Lowercase
Letters**

Alphabet
Awareness

EMC 3336

© Evan-Moor Corp.

**Matches All
Uppercase and
Lowercase
Letters**

Alphabet
Awareness

EMC 3336

© Evan-Moor Corp.

**Matches All
Uppercase and
Lowercase
Letters**

Alphabet
Awareness

EMC 3336

© Evan-Moor Corp.

**Matches All
Uppercase and
Lowercase
Letters**

Alphabet
Awareness

EMC 3336

© Evan-Moor Corp.

**Matches All
Uppercase and
Lowercase
Letters**

Alphabet
Awareness

EMC 3336

© Evan-Moor Corp.

**Matches All
Uppercase and
Lowercase
Letters**

Alphabet
Awareness

EMC 3336

© Evan-Moor Corp.

**Matches All
Uppercase and
Lowercase
Letters**

Alphabet
Awareness

EMC 3336

© Evan-Moor Corp.

**Matches All
Uppercase and
Lowercase
Letters**

Alphabet
Awareness

EMC 3336

© Evan-Moor Corp.

**Matches All
Uppercase and
Lowercase
Letters**

Alphabet
Awareness

EMC 3336

© Evan-Moor Corp.

**Matches All
Uppercase and
Lowercase
Letters**

Alphabet
Awareness

EMC 3336

© Evan-Moor Corp.

**Matches All
Uppercase and
Lowercase
Letters**

Alphabet
Awareness

EMC 3336

© Evan-Moor Corp.

**Matches All
Uppercase and
Lowercase
Letters**

Alphabet
Awareness

EMC 3336

© Evan-Moor Corp.

**Matches All
Uppercase and
Lowercase
Letters**

Alphabet
Awareness

EMC 3336

© Evan-Moor Corp.

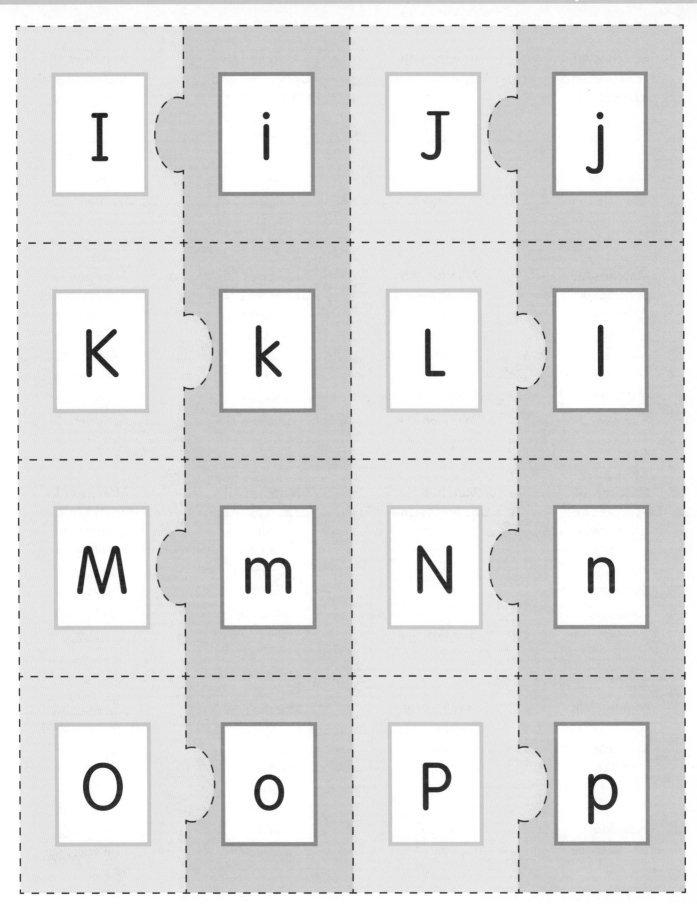

**Matches All
Uppercase and
Lowercase
Letters**

Alphabet
Awareness

EMC 3336

© Evan-Moor Corp.

**Matches All
Uppercase and
Lowercase
Letters**

Alphabet
Awareness

EMC 3336

© Evan-Moor Corp.

**Matches All
Uppercase and
Lowercase
Letters**

Alphabet
Awareness

EMC 3336

© Evan-Moor Corp.

**Matches All
Uppercase and
Lowercase
Letters**

Alphabet
Awareness

EMC 3336

© Evan-Moor Corp.

**Matches All
Uppercase and
Lowercase
Letters**

Alphabet
Awareness

EMC 3336

© Evan-Moor Corp.

**Matches All
Uppercase and
Lowercase
Letters**

Alphabet
Awareness

EMC 3336

© Evan-Moor Corp.

**Matches All
Uppercase and
Lowercase
Letters**

Alphabet
Awareness

EMC 3336

© Evan-Moor Corp.

**Matches All
Uppercase and
Lowercase
Letters**

Alphabet
Awareness

EMC 3336

© Evan-Moor Corp.

**Matches All
Uppercase and
Lowercase
Letters**

Alphabet
Awareness

EMC 3336

© Evan-Moor Corp.

**Matches All
Uppercase and
Lowercase
Letters**

Alphabet
Awareness

EMC 3336

© Evan-Moor Corp.

**Matches All
Uppercase and
Lowercase
Letters**

Alphabet
Awareness

EMC 3336

© Evan-Moor Corp.

**Matches All
Uppercase and
Lowercase
Letters**

Alphabet
Awareness

EMC 3336

© Evan-Moor Corp.

**Matches All
Uppercase and
Lowercase
Letters**

Alphabet
Awareness

EMC 3336

© Evan-Moor Corp.

**Matches All
Uppercase and
Lowercase
Letters**

Alphabet
Awareness

EMC 3336

© Evan-Moor Corp.

**Matches All
Uppercase and
Lowercase
Letters**

Alphabet
Awareness

EMC 3336

© Evan-Moor Corp.

**Matches All
Uppercase and
Lowercase
Letters**

Alphabet
Awareness

EMC 3336

© Evan-Moor Corp.

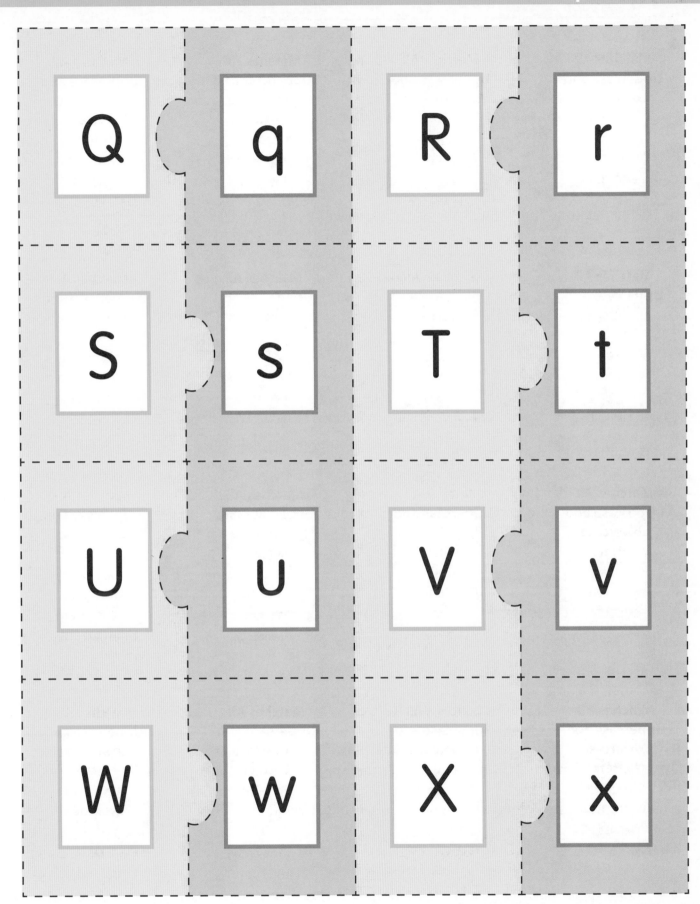

Alphabet Awareness
Matches All Uppercase and Lowercase Letters

Matches All Uppercase and Lowercase Letters

Alphabet Awareness

EMC 3336

© Evan-Moor Corp.

Matches All Uppercase and Lowercase Letters

Alphabet Awareness

EMC 3336

© Evan-Moor Corp.

Matches All Uppercase and Lowercase Letters

Alphabet Awareness

EMC 3336

© Evan-Moor Corp.

Matches All Uppercase and Lowercase Letters

Alphabet Awareness

EMC 3336

© Evan-Moor Corp.

Matches All Uppercase and Lowercase Letters

Alphabet Awareness

EMC 3336

© Evan-Moor Corp.

Matches All Uppercase and Lowercase Letters

Alphabet Awareness

EMC 3336

© Evan-Moor Corp.

Matches All Uppercase and Lowercase Letters

Alphabet Awareness

EMC 3336

© Evan-Moor Corp.

Matches All Uppercase and Lowercase Letters

Alphabet Awareness

EMC 3336

© Evan-Moor Corp.

Matches All Uppercase and Lowercase Letters

Alphabet Awareness

EMC 3336

© Evan-Moor Corp.

Matches All Uppercase and Lowercase Letters

Alphabet Awareness

EMC 3336

© Evan-Moor Corp.

Matches All Uppercase and Lowercase Letters

Alphabet Awareness

EMC 3336

© Evan-Moor Corp.

Matches All Uppercase and Lowercase Letters

Alphabet Awareness

EMC 3336

© Evan-Moor Corp.

Matches All Uppercase and Lowercase Letters

Alphabet Awareness

EMC 3336

© Evan-Moor Corp.

Matches All Uppercase and Lowercase Letters

Alphabet Awareness

EMC 3336

© Evan-Moor Corp.

Matches All Uppercase and Lowercase Letters

Alphabet Awareness

EMC 3336

© Evan-Moor Corp.

Matches All Uppercase and Lowercase Letters

Alphabet Awareness

EMC 3336

© Evan-Moor Corp.

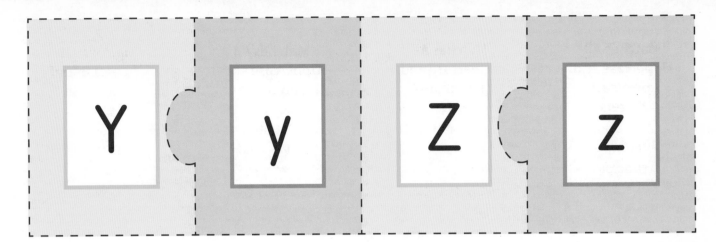

Alphabet Awareness
Matches All Uppercase and Lowercase Letters **95**

**Matches All
Uppercase and
Lowercase
Letters**

Alphabet
Awareness

EMC 3336

© Evan-Moor Corp.

**Matches All
Uppercase and
Lowercase
Letters**

Alphabet
Awareness

EMC 3336

© Evan-Moor Corp.

**Matches All
Uppercase and
Lowercase
Letters**

Alphabet
Awareness

EMC 3336

© Evan-Moor Corp.

**Matches All
Uppercase and
Lowercase
Letters**

Alphabet
Awareness

EMC 3336

© Evan-Moor Corp.

Matches All Uppercase and Lowercase Letters

Class Checklist		Record any letters that the student matched incorrectly.	
Name	Date	Letters Matched Incorrectly	Notes

Alphabet Awareness

Name _____

Match It!

Match the big letter to the little letter.

A •		• c
M •		• f
C •		• a
P •		• p
F •		• m

Checks

Unit 4
Sound Symbol Awareness

Identifies Letter and Sound

Objective:

Student says each letter name and orally produces the phonetic sound.

Materials:

Mats, pp. 103–109

Class Checklist, p. 111

Activity Sheet, p. 112

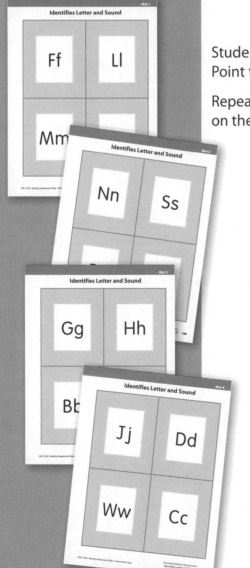

Student Task

Place mat 1 on the table. Say:

> I will point to a letter, and you say the name and the sound it makes. Let's begin.

Point to the letter *f.* Say:

> What letter is this?

Student responds. Say:

> What sound does it make?

Student responds. Record the student's response on the class checklist. Point to the next letter. Repeat the questions modeled above.

Repeat the procedure and the script modeled above for each of the letters on the remaining mats.

Identifies Letter and Sound

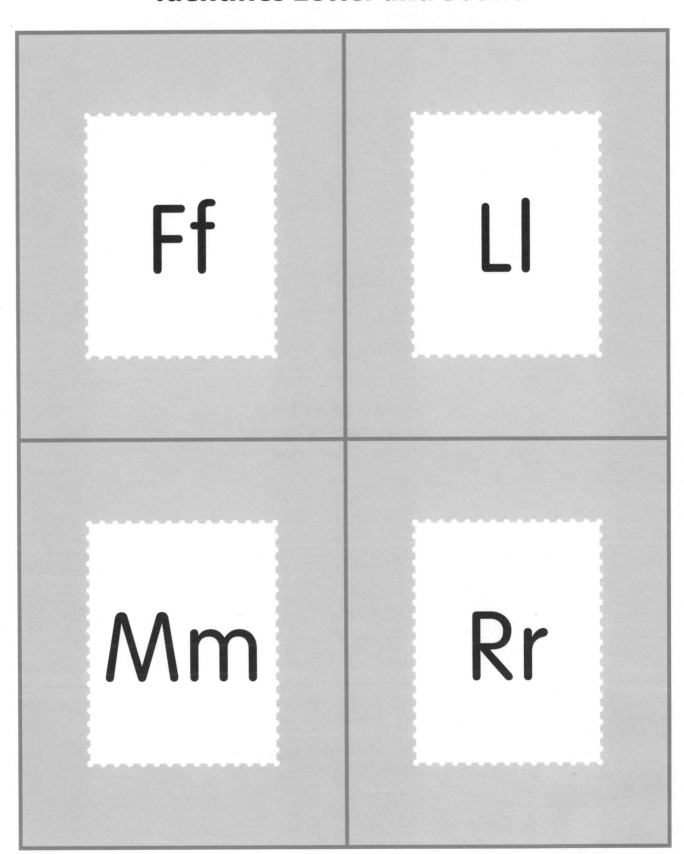

Identifies Letter and Sound

Sound Symbol Awareness

EMC 3336 • © Evan-Moor Corp.

Identifies Letter and Sound

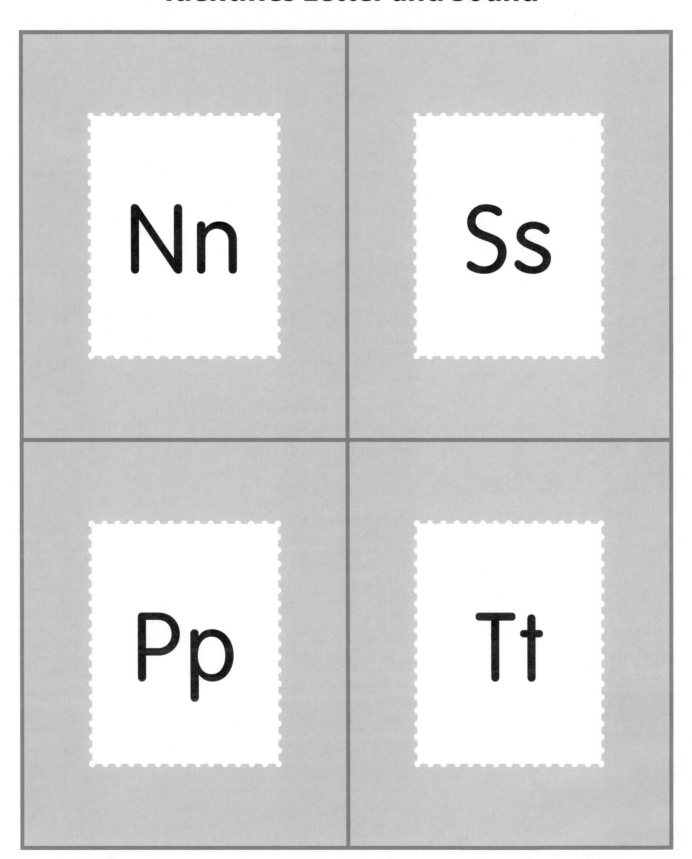

Identifies Letter and Sound

Sound Symbol Awareness

EMC 3336 • © Evan-Moor Corp.

Identifies Letter and Sound

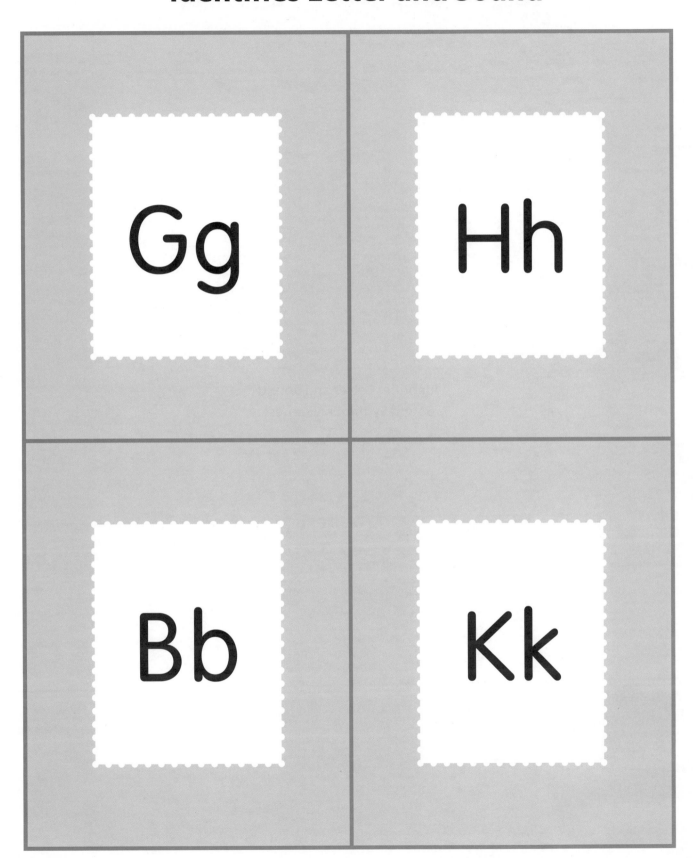

Identifies Letter and Sound
Sound Symbol Awareness

EMC 3336 • © Evan-Moor Corp.

Identifies Letter and Sound

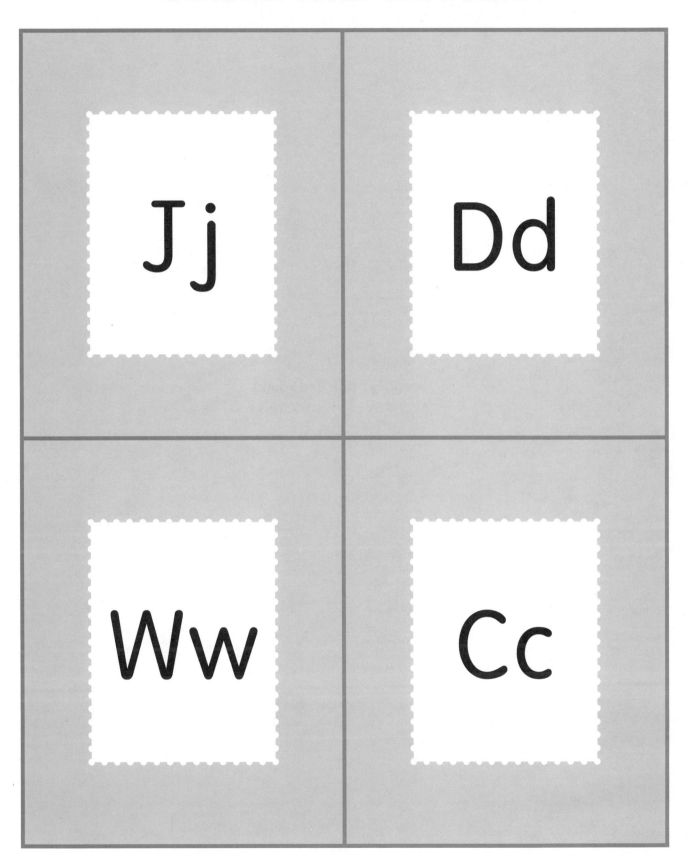

Sound Symbol Awareness
Identifies Letter and Sound **109**

Identifies Letter and Sound

Sound Symbol Awareness

EMC 3336 • © Evan-Moor Corp.

Identifies Letter and Sound

Class Checklist		Key: + correct response	− incorrect response	● self-corrected												
		Mat 1				Mat 2				Mat 3				Mat 4			
Name	Date	f	l	m	r	n	s	p	t	g	h	b	k	j	d	w	c

Sound Symbol Awareness
Identifies Letter and Sound

Note: Student names the letter and draws a line to the picture with the same sound.

Name _____

B **is for**

Name each letter.
Draw a line to the picture with the same sound.

 •   •

 •   •

 •   •

 •   •

Sound Symbol Awareness
Identifies Letter and Sound

EMC 3336 • Reading Assessment Tasks • © Evan-Moor Corp.

Matches Beginning Sound and Letter

Objective:
Student matches each beginning sound with a letter.

Materials:
Mats, pp. 115–121
Letter Cards, pp. 123–127
Class Checklist, p. 129
Activity Sheet, p. 130

Model the Task

Place mat 1 on the table. Lay the letter cards faceup in order and in rows on the table. Say:

> Today we will listen for the beginning sound in a word. Then we will find the letter that makes the beginning sound. Watch how I do it.

Point to the picture of the bike on the mat. Say:

> *Bike.* I hear /b/ at the beginning of *bike.*

Place the letter *b* card next to the picture of the bike. Say:

> The letter *b* makes the /b/ sound.

Student Task

Point to the picture of the duck on the mat. Say:

> Now it's your turn. *Duck.* What sound do you hear at the beginning of *duck?*

Student responds. Say:

> Choose the letter that makes that sound and put it next to the duck.

Student responds. Record the student's response on the class checklist. Point to the picture of the feather. Say:

> *Feather.* What sound do you hear at the beginning of *feather?*

Student responds. Say:

> Choose the letter that makes that sound and put it next to the feather.

It is important to say each picture name for the student in order to model correct pronunciation. Repeat the procedure and the script modeled above with each of the mats. Not all the letter cards will be used.

Matches Beginning Sound and Letter

Sound Symbol Awareness
Matches Beginning Sound and Letter **115**

Matches Beginning Sound and Letter

Sound Symbol Awareness

EMC 3336 • © Evan-Moor Corp.

Matches Beginning Sound and Letter

Sound Symbol Awareness
Matches Beginning Sound and Letter   **117**

Matches Beginning Sound and Letter

Sound Symbol Awareness

EMC 3336 • © Evan-Moor Corp.

Matches Beginning Sound and Letter

Sound Symbol Awareness
Matches Beginning Sound and Letter   **119**

Matches Beginning Sound and Letter

Sound Symbol Awareness

EMC 3336 • © Evan-Moor Corp.

Matches Beginning Sound and Letter

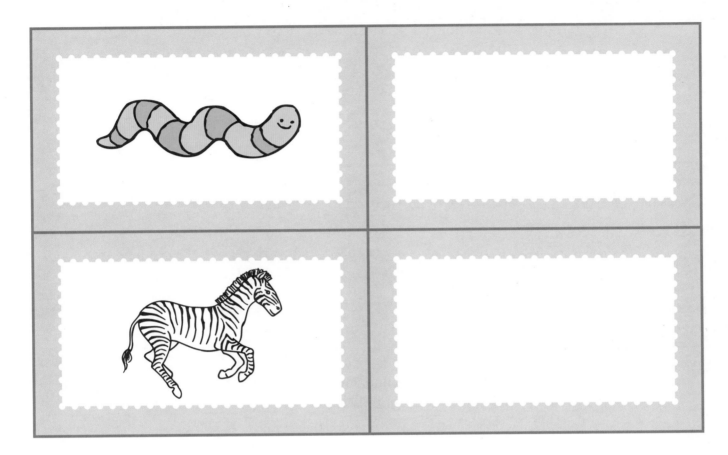

Sound Symbol Awareness
Matches Beginning Sound and Letter   **121**

Matches Beginning Sound and Letter

Sound Symbol Awareness

EMC 3336 • © Evan-Moor Corp.

b

h

d

l

f

m

Matches Beginning Sound and Letter
Sound Symbol Awareness

EMC 3336 • © Evan-Moor Corp.

Matches Beginning Sound and Letter
Sound Symbol Awareness

EMC 3336 • © Evan-Moor Corp.

Matches Beginning Sound and Letter
Sound Symbol Awareness

EMC 3336 • © Evan-Moor Corp.

Matches Beginning Sound and Letter
Sound Symbol Awareness

EMC 3336 • © Evan-Moor Corp.

Matches Beginning Sound and Letter
Sound Symbol Awareness

EMC 3336 • © Evan-Moor Corp.

Matches Beginning Sound and Letter
Sound Symbol Awareness

EMC 3336 • © Evan-Moor Corp.

g

p

r

s

t

v

Matches Beginning Sound and Letter

Sound Symbol Awareness

EMC 3336 • © Evan-Moor Corp.

Matches Beginning Sound and Letter

Sound Symbol Awareness

EMC 3336 • © Evan-Moor Corp.

Matches Beginning Sound and Letter

Sound Symbol Awareness

EMC 3336 • © Evan-Moor Corp.

Matches Beginning Sound and Letter

Sound Symbol Awareness

EMC 3336 • © Evan-Moor Corp.

Matches Beginning Sound and Letter

Sound Symbol Awareness

EMC 3336 • © Evan-Moor Corp.

Matches Beginning Sound and Letter

Sound Symbol Awareness

EMC 3336 • © Evan-Moor Corp.

y

z

x

j

w

n

Matches Beginning Sound and Letter
Sound Symbol Awareness

EMC 3336 • © Evan-Moor Corp.

Matches Beginning Sound and Letter
Sound Symbol Awareness

EMC 3336 • © Evan-Moor Corp.

Matches Beginning Sound and Letter
Sound Symbol Awareness

EMC 3336 • © Evan-Moor Corp.

Matches Beginning Sound and Letter
Sound Symbol Awareness

EMC 3336 • © Evan-Moor Corp.

Matches Beginning Sound and Letter
Sound Symbol Awareness

EMC 3336 • © Evan-Moor Corp.

Matches Beginning Sound and Letter
Sound Symbol Awareness

EMC 3336 • © Evan-Moor Corp.

Matches Beginning Sound and Letter

Class Checklist		Key: + correct response − incorrect response ● self-corrected	
Name	Date	Letters Matched Incorrectly	Notes

Name _____

Listen for the Sound

Name each picture.
Which sound do you hear at the beginning?
Fill in the circle.

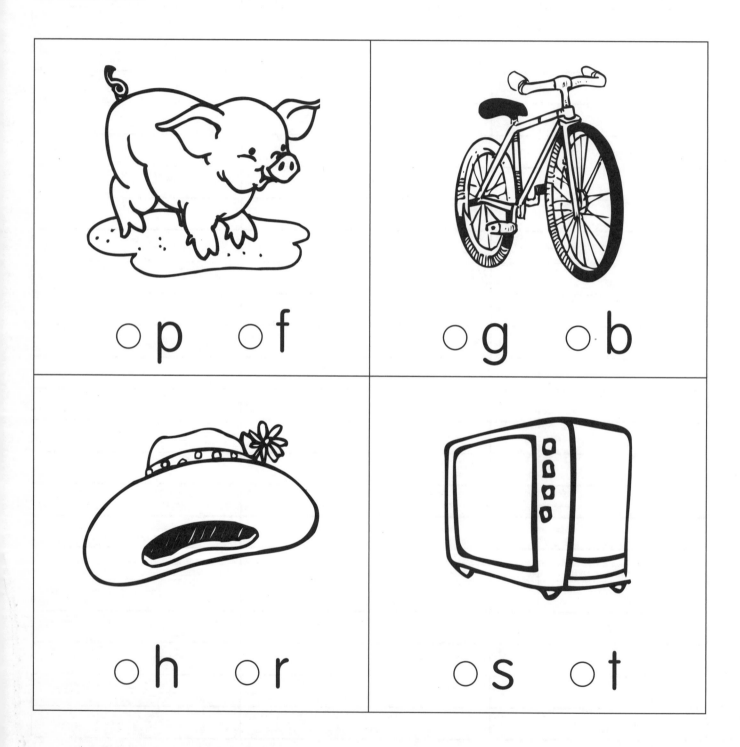

○ p   ○ f   ○ g   ○ b

○ h   ○ r   ○ s   ○ t

Checks

Unit 5

Vocabulary and Concept Development

Demonstrates Basic Knowledge

Objective:

Student provides personal information (name, address, phone number) and names the days of the week in order.

Materials:

Class Checklist, p. 135

Activity Sheet, p. 136

Auditory Only

Student Task

Have the student's personal information, such as name and address, available in order to identify responses as correct or incorrect. Say:

> Today I am going to ask you to tell me some things about yourself.

> Tell me your full name.

Student responds. Record the student's response on the class checklist. Say:

> Now tell me your address.

Student responds. Record the student's response on the class checklist. Say:

> Tell me your phone number.

Student responds. Record the student's response on the class checklist. Say:

> Now we are going to talk about the days of the week.

> Name the days of the week for me. Start with Sunday.

Student responds. Record the student's response on the class checklist.

Vocabulary and Concept Development
Demonstrates Basic Knowledge

Demonstrates Basic Knowledge

Class Checklist		Key: + correct response − incorrect response ● self-corrected				
Name	Date	Knows Name	Knows Address	Knows Phone #	Knows Days of the Week	Notes

Vocabulary and Concept Development
Demonstrates Basic Knowledge   **135**

Name _____

Me

Draw a picture of yourself.
Write your name.

_____

- - - - - - - - - - - - - - - - - - -

_____

Categorizes Objects

Objective:

Student sorts picture cards into categories on the mat.

Materials:

Mat, p. 139

Picture Cards, p. 141

Class Checklist, p. 143

Activity Sheet, p. 144

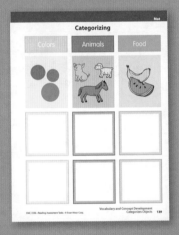

Student Task

Place the mat on the table. Lay the picture cards faceup in random order and in rows. Say:

> Things that are alike can be put into a group. For example, a lollipop, cotton candy, and a chocolate bar belong in the candy group.

Point to the picture cards. Say:

> We are going to put these pictures into groups on the mat.

Point to the mat. Say:

> This is the color group. This is the animal group, and this is the food group.

> Look at the pictures and put them into a group on the mat.

Student may sort cards into groups at his or her own pace. Use the mat as a reference to record the student's responses on the class checklist.

Vocabulary and Concept Development
Categorizes Objects

Categorizing

Colors	Animals	Food

Categorizes Objects
Vocabulary and Concept Development

EMC 3336 • © Evan-Moor Corp.

Categorizes Objects
Vocabulary and Concept
Development

EMC 3336 • © Evan-Moor Corp.

Categorizes Objects
Vocabulary and Concept
Development

EMC 3336 • © Evan-Moor Corp.

Categorizes Objects
Vocabulary and Concept
Development

EMC 3336 • © Evan-Moor Corp.

Categorizes Objects
Vocabulary and Concept
Development

EMC 3336 • © Evan-Moor Corp.

Categorizes Objects
Vocabulary and Concept
Development

EMC 3336 • © Evan-Moor Corp.

Categorizes Objects
Vocabulary and Concept
Development

EMC 3336 • © Evan-Moor Corp.

Categorizes Objects

Class Checklist		Key: + correct response − incorrect response ● self-corrected			
Name	Date	Colors	Animals	Food	Notes

Vocabulary and Concept Development
Categorizes Objects

Note: Student glues the pictures under the category of *home* or *school*.

Name _____

Where Do I Belong?

Cut and glue.

home

school

glue	glue
glue	glue
glue	glue

Understands Positional Words

Objective:

Student demonstrates an understanding of *on*, *under*, *by* (next to), and *in*.

Materials:

Mat, p. 147

Picture Cards, p. 149

Class Checklist, p. 151

Activity Sheet, p. 152

Student Task

Place the mat on the table. Place the picture cards faceup in a row on the table. Point to the mat when you talk about it. Point to the picture cards when you talk about them. Say:

> Today I am going to ask you to take the picture cards and place them somewhere on the mat. Listen carefully. Let's begin.

> Put the bird *under* the sun.

Student responds. Record the student's response on the class checklist. Say:

> Put the crab *on* the rock.

Student responds. Record the student's response on the class checklist. Say:

> Put the sea star *by* (next to) the girl.

Student responds. Record the student's response on the class checklist. Say:

> Put the fish *in* the water.

Student responds. Record the student's response on the class checklist.

Vocabulary and Concept Development
Understands Positional Words

Understands Positional Words
Vocabulary and Concept Development

EMC 3336 • © Evan-Moor Corp.

**Understands
Positional Words**

Vocabulary and
Concept Development

EMC 3336
© Evan-Moor Corp.

**Understands
Positional Words**

Vocabulary and
Concept Development

EMC 3336 • © Evan-Moor Corp.

**Understands
Positional Words**

Vocabulary and
Concept Development

EMC 3336
© Evan-Moor Corp.

**Understands
Positional Words**

Vocabulary and
Concept
Development

EMC 3336
© Evan-Moor Corp.

Understands Positional Words

Class Checklist		Key: + correct response		− incorrect response		• self-corrected
Name	Date	Under	On	By	In	Notes

Note: Student circles the word *in*, *on*, or *by* to tell where the octopus is.

Name _____

In, On, or By?

Circle the word that tells where you see the octopus.

in   on   by

in   on   by

in   on   by

in   on   by

Unit 6
Comprehension

EMC 3336 • Reading Assessment Tasks • © Evan-Moor Corp.

Understands Story Structure

Objective:

Student demonstrates an understanding of the beginning and end of a story, who the characters are in a story, how to retell a story, and how to make reasonable predictions about a story.

Materials:

Book: *Clean It Up!*, pp. 157–162

Class Checklist, p. 163

Activity Sheet, p. 164

Student Task

Seat the student next to you. Give the student a clear view of the book. Allow the student to view the cover of the book. Say:

> Listen while I read you a story called *Clean It Up!* First, let's look at the front cover. What do you think the story is about?

Student responds. Reasonable predictions include references to a family, a beach, or cleaning up a beach. Say:

> Okay, now I'll read the story to you.

Read the student *Clean It Up!* Once you have completed the story, say:

> Who was in the story?

Student responds. Say:

> Tell me what happened at the beginning of the story.

Student responds.

> Tell me what happened at the end of the story.

Student responds. Record the student's responses on the class checklist.

Clean It Up!

Tanya and her family went to the beach
for a picnic.
The beach had a lot of trash.
It was a mess.

Tanya's mom said,
"Let's clean it up!"

Everyone helped.

Jamal and Kim picked up paper.
Tanya picked up bottles.
Mom and Dad picked up soda cans.

The beach is finally clean.
Now they can have a picnic.

The End

Understands Story Structure

Class Checklist		Key: + correct response − incorrect response ● self-corrected				
Name	Date	Makes Reasonable Predictions	Identifies Characters	Beginning of Story	End of Story	Notes

Name _____

1, 2, 3

Color. Cut. Glue in order.

1
2
3

Comprehension
Understands Story Structure

Objective:

Student places pictures in sequential order on the mat.

Materials:

Mat, p. 167

Picture Cards, p. 169

Class Checklist, p. 171

Activity Sheet, p. 172

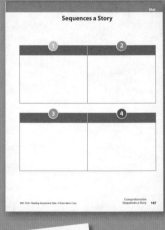

Student Task

Place the mat on the table. Place the picture cards faceup in random order and in a row. Say:

> Look at the pictures. Each picture tells part of a story. We are going to put the pictures in order to tell the story. Let's begin.

> Choose the picture you think is first in the story. Put it in box 1 on the mat.

Student responds. Say:

> Now choose the next picture in the story and put it in box 2 on the mat.

Student responds. Say:

> Finish the story. Put the next two pictures in boxes 3 and 4 on the mat.

Use the mat as a reference to record the student's responses on the class checklist.

Sequences a Story

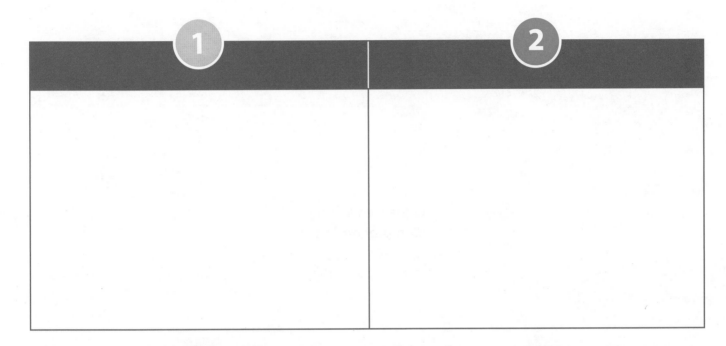

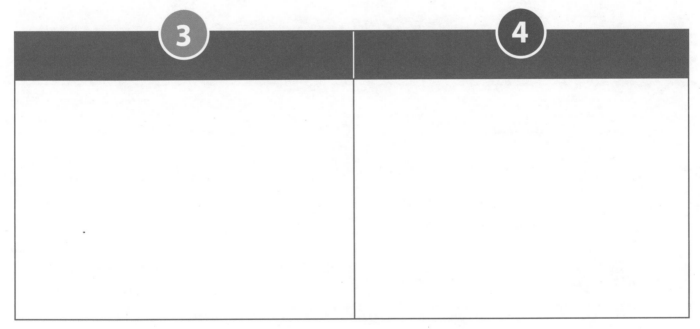

Sequences a Story

Comprehension

EMC 3336 • © Evan-Moor Corp.

Sequences a Story

Comprehension

EMC 3336 • © Evan-Moor Corp.

Sequences a Story

Comprehension

EMC 3336 • © Evan-Moor Corp.

Sequences a Story

Comprehension

EMC 3336 • © Evan-Moor Corp.

Sequences a Story

Comprehension

EMC 3336 • © Evan-Moor Corp.

Sequences a Story

Class Checklist		Key: **+** correct response − incorrect response ● self-corrected	
Name	Date	Sequences Story	Notes

Name _____

Make a Snowman

Draw what happens next.

Answer Key

Page 20

Page 26

Page 42

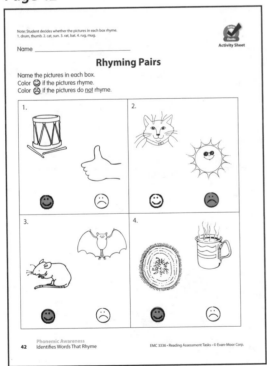

Page 48

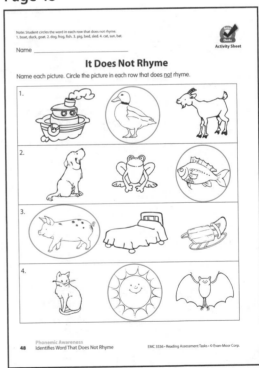

Page 58

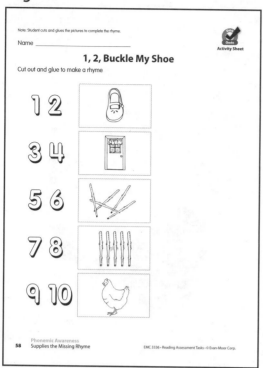

Page 64

Page 70

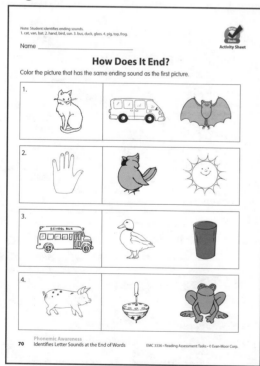

Page 76

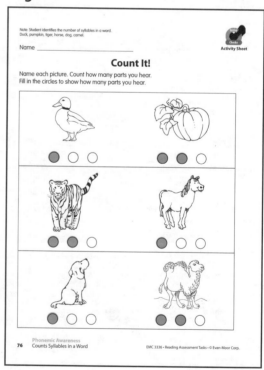

Page 98

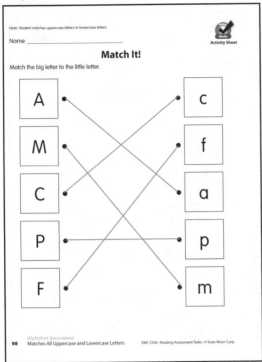

Name _____

Match It!

Match the big letter to the little letter.

A — c
M — f
C — a
P — p
F — m

Page 112

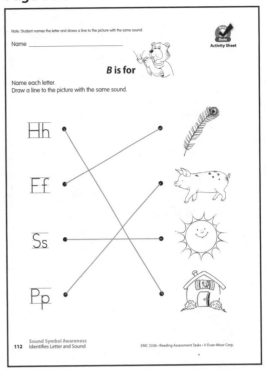

Name _____

B is for

Name each letter.
Draw a line to the picture with the same sound.

Hh
Ff
Ss
Pp

Page 130

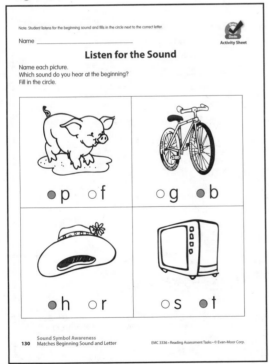

Name _____

Listen for the Sound

Name each picture.
Which sound do you hear at the beginning?
Fill in the circle.

● p   ○ f   ○ g   ● b

● h   ○ r   ○ s   ● t

Page 136

Name _____

Me

Draw a picture of yourself.
Write your name.

Answers will vary.

Page 144

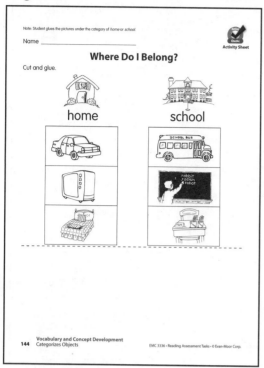

Where Do I Belong?

Cut and glue.

home   school

Note: Student glues the pictures under the category of *home* or *school*.

Name _____

Vocabulary and Concept Development
Categorizes Objects

EMC 3336 • Reading Assessment Tasks • © Evan-Moor Corp.

Page 152

In, On, or By?

in   on   by

Circle the word that tells where you see the octopus.

(in)   on   by   in   (on)   by

in   on   (by)   (in)   on   by

Note: Student circles the word *in*, *on*, or *by* to tell where the octopus is.

Name _____

Vocabulary and Concept Development
Understands Positional Words

EMC 3336 • Reading Assessment Tasks • © Evan-Moor Corp.

Page 164

1, 2, 3

Color. Cut. Glue in order.

Note: Student cuts and glues to put the pictures in order.

Name _____

Comprehension
Understands Story Structure

EMC 3336 • Reading Assessment Tasks • © Evan-Moor Corp.

Page 172

Make a Snowman

Draw what happens next.

1.   2.

3.   4.

Drawings will vary.

Note: Student draws a picture to tell what happens next.

Name _____

Comprehension
Sequences a Story

EMC 3336 • Reading Assessment Tasks • © Evan-Moor Corp.